Saltwater Empire

POETRY

Raymond McDaniel

COFFEE HOUSE PRESS
MINNEAPOLIS
2008

COFFEE HOUSE PRESS books are available to the trade through our primary distributor, Consortium Book Sales & Distribution, www.cbsd.com or (800) 283-3572. For personal orders, catalogs, or other information, write to: Coffee House Press, 27 North Fourth Street, Suite 400, Minneapolis, MN 55401.

Coffee House Press is a nonprofit literary publishing house. Support from private foundations, corporate giving programs, government programs, and generous individuals helps make the publication of our books possible. We gratefully acknowledge their support in detail in the back of this book.

To you and our many readers around the world, we send
our thanks for your continuing support.

LIBRARY OF CONGRESS CIP INFORMATION
Library of Congress Cataloging-in-Publication Data

McDaniel, Raymond, 1969–
Saltwater empire : poems / by Ray McDaniel.
p. cm.
ISBN-13: 978-1-56689-213-1 (alk. paper)
ISBN-10: 1-56689-206-6
I. Title.
PS3613.C3868S35 2008
811'.6—DC22
FIRST EDITION | FIRST PRINTING

1 3 5 7 9 8 6 4 2
PRINTED IN THE U.S.A.

ACKNOWLEDGMENTS

Many thanks to the following periodicals in which versions of these poems appeared, sometimes in different forms: *The Boston Review, The Canary, The Hat, Spinning Jenny, Conduit, Pindledyboz, From the Fishouse,* and *Michigan Today Audio Archive.*

The text of the "Convention Centers of the New World" poems is drawn from interviews conducted by volunteers for Alive in Truth: the New Orleans Disaster Oral History & Memory Project, which records life histories of people from New Orleans, Louisiana, and nearby areas who were affected by Hurricane Katrina. I have assembled the poems by recombining several of these histories, and I offer my deepest gratitude to the interviewees and to the project organizers and volunteers. For more information about Alive in Truth, including opportunities to donate to the organization so that it can continue to preserve the voices of the Gulf Coast, please visit their website at www.aliveintruth.org.

SALTWATER EMPIRE

CONTENTS

SEA LEVEL

To know what element of air is unruly rain.

What of your weight is wept or lost to sweat.

What water can be caught in a photograph folded half
    and half again.

    what witchery remains in a standing piano
    what room for choruses before they become other people's music
    what innocence perseveres in boxcars buried beneath sea level
    what accelerates a train so that it skips like a stone
        from St. George's to Port-au-Prince
    what then-excellence is the experience of sleep
        on a bed of old guitar strings
    what of infinite curses forks a tongue, what silvers one
    of what salt measure is made the rollicking mercury
        of our blood pitch-blackened
    what fall from a treehouse constitutes providence
    what churches predestine
    what sight gravesites a thumbprint
    what symmetry speaks lemongrass and mint
    what establishes balance with date palms
        and the almond-dull bell of a trumpet

Sing, stomp.

Miscalculate, mister, whistle and divide.

Cross and tune. Undo.

To know what you must swallow from the corners
    of this photograph:

sip, mister,

then drink. Drink, so not to drown.

MISTER

Note pinned to the bruiser's breast

ragman   stick wrist   bark cured clean

shape of a man   crucifix   god of wheat

hanged man's hood   husk tongue   speak

Emperor Atibon, Professor-I-Told-You-So,
signified that unlucky fool
        with an arrow through his figurehead heart.
If that don't show you what will?

        Wrote in your old room, you remember
all that nonsense, dead ferns and root beer bottles,
        cheap burgundy cloth.
love you xoxox

jack in the grass   armature's broken back

dumbed doll   cheating puppet   my prank

patchwork thing   mere thing   tatterdemalion

        O little man, little man I've made

SCRATCH

scratch   name of a deal poorly made

your scrap violin

only later   now say   who you were chasing

(who was chasing who was chasing you)

through the palmetto and sawgrass

across forehead   down cheek split

vine-caressed letter   scrub whip stitched

what goes   solo   no devil like an old one

that x

black bead crusted   crescent along the thread

he who gave you that confusion   wound to tissue

to head

barracks of gods   little spitting gods

instrument abraded   scratch of the devil

(unclean)

his hate the trace   of where you've been

SLEEPERS

Solid walls, deliquesce. Solid worlds, wake.

Radio souls, drop your brass to the tracks, lock your notes
    to their heavens or havens.

Sailors, lace yourselves to stations, for the underwater railroad
    makes fluid freight.

For our train, subaqueous, delivers men and mails by coral trestle.

The shifting tonnage shuffles up waves of pure bass, a cardiac click.

The engine's bellow a promise made, then marred.

Impeccable grade, graphite and black, wheels unneeded,
    its windows thin.

Our age's ache is only that train's liquid weight, heard from far off,
    too long gone, on its way.

Our underwater railroad carves its unknown road, its divine tide.

Sleepers, occupy this impossible, onerous weight,
    hastened to some other place.

Each past moment a chamber that cannot be entered,

    its prior crushed just.

Our black train's tunnels slump into flood.

Afterimage of our underwater railroad, its tracks elapse

    phosphorescent.

FREQUENCY MODULATION

you are listening to

the transmission via seed pearl, aural irritant

clockwork and sparkgap ultra high and superlow

precious black opal crystal and glass shudders and sings

broad cast scattered the seeds among the apocrypha

each agent at land or sea satellite or space

direct conversion of royal register and groove

high in fidelity to

our regenerative radio hisses and shouts

everything that cannot be owned belongs now to us

irradiant waves oscillate below visible light

to arrive and reside requires no medium but occupies vacuum

and air transformational emission

follow your radiotelegraph

we are your conductor our amplitude varies

we fluctuate the frequency

we are not subject to static interference

we embed the subcarrier

hush y'all

you need not know that language if you know this sound

A LA INDIGENES

more of us:

here's our girlhood and boyhood
our godlets and godawful

here's
the hottest shit on wax

and how we became *I am a grown-ass man*
held in common

how we became sea-breathers & or versus weredogs
fishermen & felonious assault
street pharmacists & or versus day laborers
cane cutters & citizens of sawgrass

a k a Jack-a-nothing
& Girl Not A *Good Got* Damn –

events subsequent, boring as fuck

ALTERNATE RECORDINGS OF STORMY WEATHER

Sometimes the soldier splits the staff.
Or the monster's tongue tells the tale.

Or fresh blossoms muster a bewitching.
Or our reach retreats to utter abandon.

The ship is magnolia, great seal of wax.
The ship builds a pulpit, a prophet, a cell.

A set whose scene is then flood.
A white tide, a storm drain.

Water's action creates a *fastness*.
It's vast, curved, unaccountable.

Hollower, harrower, it dirties as it sweeps.
Our faults are staggering, our geology.

Our earth disuses her fossils in flood.
Her limited force is still a demon.

A tempest is certain serpentine.
A tempest is awful appetite.

Rains promise a prescient bombardment.
First the scrim, the hue of rain.

Then the stage, the wreck of rain.
Then the cast of rain, its players.

Flesh and circumstance of rain,
speech of ensorcelled rain.

Serenaded. Swooned to.
Full fathom five thy father lies –

Sorcerer sister dearest daughter spirit slave.
Mortal, which are you.

PEDIGREE

I got a hundred cousins

the boys could seduce the pit out of a cherry

but those girls, straightrazors every one

they'll cut you right up

"tattoos while you wait!!"

my very own crackers, *please*

you want a fight

fight me

ZOMBI PHENOTYPES

Pit means flood. To bury is to drown.

Mosquito netting's opera lace for godly, for godlets.

Only flesh can masquerade mechanical.

Timorous, shopworn glamour, we walkaround.

We hold hands, embrace prettily.

Amazers, all gone down, a drowned township.

Unfleshed, enchanted skeletons.

We issue with 300 bones and while away to 206.

Suit up, sisters, suit up, sailors.

Whose lips are sewn shut with this prickly thread?

And will one day die down, unhinged comportment.

Ossuary-postured unless so ensorcelled even our shape sings.

is they is or is they ain't

You see in your mind the swamp god seize his own skeleton.

He pulls it, shining white, from the muck.

But in truth the tannin bleaches the bones black.

CONVENTION CENTERS OF THE NEW WORLD

I come from all over New Orleans. What I feel needs to be said
about this is that everything was done wrong.

From what I can see, the police could not control the crime
in New Orleans. Before the floods and the hurricane.

I do have a church home, Greater St. Matthews Baptist Church.
I've been a member there since 1969.

That's pretty much that's how it is. Every person from New Orleans,
their family has been there.

Not everybody from New Orleans is bad. Some good people come
from New Orleans, but it's just the way they train people in New Orleans.

In 1990 I moved into Magnolia Housing Project.
They call it the CJ Peete housing project now.

I live on Milan Street, and I'm like one, two blocks
from Napoleon Avenue, the street where rich people stay.

You all might see a lot of people with dreadlocks in their hair.
You don't have to be scared.

It kind of like became a religion in New Orleans,
so y'all don't have be scared when you see long hair.

When I was staying with my grandmother, Ms. Amelia,
it was 2256 1/2 Trevor Street.

In New Orleans, you be lucky if you had money to go
to Payless Shoes and get you some shoes

and find something cheap to dress up in.
And it look more better than a $200 or $300 dress.

I liked my house in New Orleans. I fixed it up nice.
Every piece of furniture I had, it came from the rental.

The man I was renting from was Aaron's on South Broad Street
in New Orleans. My agent was Greg.

I had a three-bedroom. I turned one room into a dining room.
I turned another room into a den. I had a bedroom.

I had a large kitchen. I had a large living room. I lived comfortably!
But I paid out for every thing I got. I rented furniture and I paid for it.

I ain't owe nobody nothing after the storm, before the storm,
during the storm, I ain't owe nobody Jack nothing.

The table and the lamps go to that living room set. I had this TV,
that's my microwave I brought back from New Orleans.

bacchus.

*

Bring a corollary rather than want a spirit

for spirits we do not lack.

Bring food for five days.

All around us wind wrinkles the water, puckers the water, ages it —

Air, the invisibles, manifested so fast our ears snapped shut.

The water fled, then, fast, the water came back.

Bye now, shy horizon.

Outpaced its own crest and collapsed.

But *of course* we preserve *the carnival.*

Drink this —

this drunkard for a god and worship.

Blaze, Pontchartrain. Sink the city to flood and fire.

Poor mourner, trail the flambeaux hem down St. Philip.

We tangle our hands in our hair.

We catch diamonds in our vascular channels.

Rote, beloved, drunk, we play connect-the-dots.

We suture the city with celebration.

PLANET MESSIAH

evil demigod type

satellite sky-god

all armor-giddy all cloud-platformed

magnifier, maker

his ship a black molecule focuses his lens rotates

his orbit funnels sunshine to fish out mermen

boils the sea to dust

leaves the copperside gasping

floats on – arch locust

cleopatra.

*

Celebrants, mortal spangle.

The sight of them splinters, glitters the goddamned eyeball.

Regents to royal, our costume carnage –

we slide down to the Marigny on sequins,

we slip past porches and children.

Each winding-back offers a narrow not only out of neighborhood.

We loiter on roofs that burned the calluses from the feet

of those left there.

Seared the prints from their fingers.

We blow soap bubbles down blocks that boiled with stray propane –

burning even underwater.

Queen Pristine, Polychrome Philistine!

The tune of our catch played by the picture.

We trod a maze trod indeed through forthrights and meanders.

Some drowned in attics for none had basements.

We make our way, our wits enameled.

Clad in feather and rainbow chrome, we undress.

THIS IS A RECORDING

Shrug off the mood but the tune cannot be escaped.
My sainted mother's song prizes
tarpaper, water's tap, shuffle of the broom on the roof
so the whole house don't fall in, precious.
No room in her room, no sound silenced,
no key unkeyed. Night was dark but the sky was blue.
Don't go nowhere. Who do you love.
Radio replaces today's weather,
lightning's white stitches up lilac and slate,
tugs clouds down to downpour.
Murder ballad and Bible book say
if x becomes abomination in thine eyes
then shut thine eyes and darkness once more
upon the water. But let the needle slip
into the acetate and there's nowhere
even God can get to, can go.
My Dixie holograms sheathe and shine.
I throw this gift down a well and praise the echo,
seed every inch of Lake Providence
with microphone until the swamp serenades
itself. That lake is the will of God, God filled it up.
That *is* what you sound like. Jesus
don't need to breathe to man the trestle and track.
That rail, underwater railroad,
each drowned station stippled with sound.
Who do you love. Who do you love.
Don't you know a railroad man will kill you if he can.

CONVENTION CENTERS OF THE NEW WORLD

Like I say about my momma: my momma she taught me
everything I need to know.

My real mother, the woman that gave me birth,
when I was small they put something in her drink.

It was the kind of stuff that goes on in New Orleans.
She went out with her own kin people

and when they brought her back home later, she just wasn't talking right.
Come to find out, somebody had put something in her drink.

You know something? My grandmother, she did voodoo.
My grandmother did voodoo.

My grandmother was – I hate to say evil,
but she was close to it, close to it.

There was six of us in the house. I was the only boy –
I had five sisters.

I come from a family of ten children.
Five girls, five boys.

Because I always was a problem child out of twelve children.
I was the eleventh child.

I have seven children myself. I seen how hard it was for my mom
and I tried to be like my mom – which I could never be.

I have five boys and two girls. All athletes except one.
One has his own business with space walks and waterslides.

As my oldest daughter got older, the girls always wanted to fight her
because she was very pretty.

But my children, they had an easy life. When I had my first child
at seventeen, I said,

"I'm going to work and I'm going to take care of my children."
My children, all of us would be sitting on the porch, they'll say,

"Oh Mama, go to the store and get me a cold drink
and a bag of potato chips." My neighbor, she'll get very angry.

"They're your children, you let them send you to the store?"
I said "I don't have nothing better to do."

If they had to go to Winn-Dixie, they'll get in the car and go.
I'll walk to Winn-Dixie.

And I am poor. I don't have a lot of money, you know.
I had an automobile – it wasn't a brand new automobile.

I had my wedding pictures in her car and the book of my wedding pictures
and some other personal stuff I had.

I'm a welder. I'm a first-class welder.
I had a job back at home working at a shipyard.

I was making $16.
in New Orleans, $16 was a lot.

I mean, we had a good life.
We never went without lights, we never went hungry.

We used to go into baseball practice,
and have regular activities.

I always if they said don't do it, I done it.
I just have to prove a point to people.

It's that if someone tell me I can't do it. . . .
I've been into it numerous times with the New Orleans police.

You know, despite of all the fighting and stuff, I never was abused
by no man. Never ever, because they knew.

They knew: keep your hands to yourself.
But I just had to show them that they could not move me.

muses.

*

A red dress hung on the girl, dirty with exotic.

Sullen, simmering.

Dressed only to strip, shop, or steal:
All we know how to do is look good.

We trawl for anything black.
We like the way it decreates skin.

Hot fraction peering from under cotton wrists.

Fashion, we laugh at the upright mirror.

I have no tits

Half pride, half bewilderment.

How do I look?

We sleep against each other on the way home.

We slip ourselves into a thick envelope of tropical rain.

We vanish strangely, we speak without opening our eyes.

Subdued rasp of interrupted dream:

Carry me   I'm tired.

CERTAIN CHILD

Satellite lights. We nick our knives
on the ship's hard mechanical teeth.
Shaving a rosed head — essence unearthed.
A graphic action, a cerise ink
to measure it — to lacerate.
No room but a glorious wall —
call civil a poor dish in a loud house.
Pendulum hours scour out our heads —
our needs. We were taught
to trust the barrel's hollow —
against the maelstrom, its mouth.

HALVED

Never enough food to spare a taste,
no treat for her little lords and ladies.

Unseen her lines and hook, her net and basket.
Unseen her feats or fealty, her brackwater catch.

She has never know a grain grown straight.
Never mind plum honey on my hands,

my stitched-up soiled fingers soiled sweet.
Her fingers splay, her roots grow in gloves,

each indictment a witch's discretion,
each night grown through the gloves,

a bulb pregnant but not yet beloved.
I desired a lemon, had no knife to cut it.

Just oil shining at her lip and the flat face
of the pan, cast iron eased with seasoning.

Cayenne pepper in my fist, all sprung,
and black pepper squared, and salt.

Cold milk cracks the sugar, blond sugar-milk
comes undone in her cup of sharp chicory.

Her blue pitcher and matching glass,
scarred spoon and fork missing a tine,

the cast iron in her hand, arm by her side,
door open to the yard, her clothesline,

her sheets dry on that line. Oranges fat
on the tree, seeds full on the sill. *Move,*

my rooms and wall and excellent lamp,
my dry rice my tin room my rain.

But Goddamn   there *was* a magnolia
it was in my very backyard   and I'm sorry to say it
there were also chickens   but fried chicken is *good*
and also watermelon parties   but watermelon is *good*
sometimes a tire swing or inner tube or the real-live river
we slipped in and out of   cut-offs and sunburns
aloe for aches and even   the moon, too,
it shone on everything   and even the moonlight
scorched everything   can I help it
having come up hard   the trash of y'all's fantasy?
To find a chassis on blocks   set in my yard
it's mine, it's my yard   square and protected
come on over   get the hell out.

COLOR MAP

Patches of seagrass resemble small plots —
gardens — garden colors. Soil on the half
landscape of your sleeve. Work taste,
roots, seed, and smudge. Soup promised.
I lifted the sleeve of my sweater —
you are always wearing my sweater —
and nothing. Washed in a whole other
race of water entire. Wrung —
slapped against flattened stones —
stiff until the dumb automatic motor —
my labor — thaws inside it.

EZILI'S REMEDY FOR RAIN

Ezilis. Our sea's the wrong god for a lover.
Inconsolable, we mix tincture, refuse petitions.

We quarantine dreams, solicit the ill, seduce
via lightning's electric spectacle, part of lips parting.

We reserve our temper for bad bad men,
tut-tut women with less luck than patience.

Folded into backyards, we tend a wife, her cut
between scratch and gash, an ebony l etched into her cheek.

Her legend letter from having erred, having bent
her head then raised it for reckoning.

We carry her to the bed of cypress roots,
to our blankets of mud and music.

She is almost sea in water lost from leaves.
She ruptures into soil where our fingers disappear her.

Motherless sisters, summoned with a serving dish,
a pig's carcass set on abalone or alabaster.

The woman murmurs a curse. Ask for a bandage
or a butterfly stitch and earn eternal aquatint.

We take her hand without glance or asking,
we strike sticks that curl into trees.

Our sea sways over her corpse's curtain,
the letter l stains her cheek, her funeral sheet.

Her child will love rattles and things that spin,
love guedhes, their paint that is blood and bead.

We survive not by force, but bliss.
Whatever you utter, your prayer becomes this.

NOW YOU

Waiting on masts – for the ocean
to smoke – to float to nothing –
nets undreamed at their corners –
perfume. Like peeling apart
a deck of cards. Signature – yours –
dropped into a room like bait.
We will set doors on the sea,
to make shade, a hole for the schools –
sometimes it's like that sometimes
it's cheating – coming back. If you
will, love, aye – forfeit me now.

GENEALOGY OF A RECURVE KISS

At the drive-in theater backlit by hurricane light
the good God allows the murders of Saint Sebastian.

Robin Hood shoots blind, then sits, rests, having chosen his grave.

Tell splits the apple.
Bushido demands a sparrow felled from horseback.
A little pink god points and says *love*.

The bow promises two points and the quickest means between them.

A kiss, a message held taut to the cheek.

So we learn to strike from a distance, then commit.

Fair in the mind of eros, which in its discipline makes perfect the
languid eye.

Or imagines the spine of a marlin strung with jade seawater.

The substance les flèches, pressed cedar or bamboo.

Arrows quickly score the quarrelsome path of undone space.

Target: all who would flee.

I got you. I got you. See.

Gesture of love, quiver spent of arsenal, of pins and letters.

A whole mottled, dappled world to map with just these lines,
any one of which could serve as an index of war.

Sebastian is also Gwan Be, flat spirit on a playing card,
protectorate of wood, house warden of this island.

He is the post, the saint, the arrow itself.

We desire and we breathe and we draw.

Quick, quick, mimic the kiss.

We loose the shaft that turns this grove to ash.

orpheus.

*

Italic riptide.

Mischief makes this island our own forever.

The river dwindles then bloats, makes brack and wreck.

Here comes the river, its ten thousand limbs.

Its very presence tearing you apart.

ASSAULT TO ABJURY

Rain commenced, and wind did.

A crippled ship slid ashore.

Our swimmer's limbs went heavy.

The sand had been flattened.

The primary dune, the secondary dune, both leveled.

The maritime forest, extracted.

Every yard of the shore was shocked with jellyfish.

The blue pillow of the man o' war empty in the afterlight.

The threads of the jellyfish, spent.

Disaster weirdly neatened the beach.

We cultivated the debris field.

Castaway trash, our treasure.

Jewel box, spoon ring, sack of rock candy.

A bicycle exoskeleton without wheels, grasshopper green.

Our dead ten speed.

We rested in red mangrove and sheltered in sheets.

Our bruises blushed backwards, our blisters did.

is it true is it true

God help us we tried to stay shattered but we just got better.

We grew adept, we caught the fish as they fled.

We skinned the fish, our knife clicked like an edict.

We were harmed, and then we healed.

SEN JAK'S ADVICE TO THE TROPICALLY DEPRESSED

As for palm-food, pinched face on the fruit
in your hands: that milk is too sweet

to be trusted. For my part I prefer lime
mingled with rum in the eddies

of this tattoo. While waiting this out,
you should eat, burn your fingers then suck them

clean, lament the singe and savor the sediment.
Not to remind you: to anchor.

Mistake a cult, fail a quiz, watch your washing
waste away to a burial. I afflict, I affix,

I wish constantly to impress. I save
sweets for my suitors, my chevaliers.

Between us we haul corpse-weight
like a pair of jackasses, tails and fates.

We bray and balk. All this costume,
it comes from theater, bespeaks bellyaches

of joy and starvation, suffers satin
and deadly serious, gasoline a bounty

no less for burning. I tinker soldiers
made of tin, rusted sailormen.

I impress upon you no clemency
but the mercy of my inhabitation.

You are all shipwreck stories. No, it is just
this room, falling into water. Of that,

even the dirt remembers. Taste the bread
we've made, hien? You, too, will have souls.

THROUGH THE SHOTGUN HOUSE, WITH VIOLINS

If y'all weren't so poor you'd know better.
Vinyl 45's or portable radio: pretenders.

Screen door, light door, horizontal chance
back-borne as burn and burden: weight

and spring to make the needle keen.
Over tangerine meat pulped on coquina

we design to prefer poise, piano-time,
each key the weight of stone disjointed.

In place of note untended, we molasses,
fixed to the seasons our limbs go lank,

awkward akimbo, collapsible. What instinct
stole us our azalea-shine? Girl, you run

like your hair was on fire. I fan my fingers
over your squint-shut eyes, mimic the epileptic

white of sunlight through palm spines.
By reverie yet irreverent thus achieve

the assumption of sulk, of seed and soil.
Ply dirt into my fingerprints, get loose

to the thieves' inch along the radio dial.
No matter, no mass, that there is no

ever-summer: all winters green
dark to depth, green to self & sugar,

coin of the cutter's world, awful faces
dust-sweetened. *You little monsters.*

Sick on mirror-water from the hose,
sick on planet seen through that water,

sinuous, indistinct as fever. I see us:
seizure shotgun from front door

to black back door of this house.
I know the occurrence of objects

in this climate. Even music, if left
to our weather, will warp within days.

NOBODY MOVES NOBODY GETS HURT

but what did you really do with whatever

you stole   didn't you burn everything you stole

I did I burned it I burned all of it

and what did you do with the cars y'all stole

didn't you drive them into the sea

didn't you leave them on the westside with the engine running

I did I took from the rich and gave to whoever the fuck

on the westside westside westside

you don't even have your own mouth to feed

you have no excuse   amateur   you deserve none

PHILOSOPHY OFFICE

Pretty slate shutters — slate door.
Books no substitute for fruit, weary,
come-hither on spring-supple, taste
of them pierced as the proposal of taste —
aujord'hui, d'accord, argent, mercredi.
With your lips slowed to language
of counsel — emperor words point
at other emperor words — like gossips
all the books swell open in the heat.
Iron Market gossips and your mouth —
sleep with me. Stay, but not here.

endymion.

*

Great guilt, like poison given to work a great time after.

Never because our feet were tired but often our head, our eyes.

Sepia, surely the worst thing that ever happened to us.

We never read the paper, we never missed our stop.

We each went to our similar houses.

Set a hand on her, whore, and see what happens –

Our sister serene, beloved of the redeemer.

Once and whereupon we fling stones against windows.

Revolt between summer tar and shotgun shutters.

We shout up – *take my picture!*

Flash hold on the slide sheet, the side street.

Now speak to us, embrace our body.

This thing of darkness, acknowledge yours.

SWAMP THING

Parthenogenerated, God comes from nowhere.
Our lord says, but also is said.
Did he or did he not feed the Boudreaux
and the sand farmers and the tatter Irish
and the poachers and the whores
with the meat of lowly, unclean beasts?
The motto of this sovereign state is *get out*
yet still the great god of the bog persists.
One day a faithless says *faggot*
to the unloved in a gas station restroom
and the next day is given to shout out
Jesus-gardens. From the bog god's scalp
spring skullcap flowers and candyweed.
The lord left the mountains and the deserts
to take the whole of Apalachicola in his mouth,
rattle the oysters under his tongue
and crack the shells between his teeth,
spit out Dixie Beer and a fine sheet of grit,
a million glass beads,
the teawater a tannic manna.
Hallelujah the halo of his hair, the frayed nimbus
a cane thrashed through cypress stands.
The rhizomes of his ringlets float filthy
in the water, mint sprigs in hot sweet tea.
His curls compress into yams,

from fistfuls of that thread grow the silver hives
of fat and savory river rats.
God grew up from fools and from under sinners,
up from the floor and under the sink,
kudzu crown that grew in a gas station bathroom
south of, get out of.
Fertile, his urine, his brine, his mud, his mind,
flesh of his harvest, sweet of his spit.
Monstrous, y'all, but effulgent.
This bark is his body, parishioner
and Philistine, this brack is his blood.

CONVENTION CENTERS OF THE NEW WORLD

I'm not perfect. I try to be perfect and what will keep
me from panicking is understanding that I could pray.

Whatever God want to hand me, He gonna want to hand me.
So that would keep me humble.

But the devil do get ahold to me sometimes.
Yeah sometimes I'll go for like two or three months,

and then I'll back away for like two or three months.
That's not good at all

because as good as God has been to me,
I need to serve him every day of the week.

This had to happen. The hurricane had to happen.
This was the way the Lord had to clean New Orleans up.

Because the police could not stop the violence, the drugs,
the murder, the robbing, the rape.

The police couldn't stop it, so that was the way for the Lord
to stop it. He wiped out what He wanted to wipe out.

But far as myself, I think the Lord has given me nine chances.
I don't have no more. I don't have no more chances with God.

I could pray but whatever God want to hand me,
He gonna want to hand me.

BOYS WITH CRUCIFIXES

Salvation. Our shoulder-blades scissoring.

Confirmation silver a pendulum and sternum, a swing.

Cured of age, boys with crucifixes carry lightly their noise.

Exit by one then exodus, balsam doors white on their backs.

Our air freight, our kite-along.

Married to a music so slow it severs.

Cleaving cells, spindle by spindle.

slow music to take us to deuces / boys with crucifixes

Shine with the vanity of plants under glass.

Folios crease not in time, but in minds.

The sun leaches the sheets to lemon-white.

A year for the wind to turn a leaf

I believed the train would whisper right through me.

IDIOCY

orange primer marks the continents
on the chassis checker cab rigid planet
interrupted with dogwood bloom
that same storm steps off ocean
northeaster nostalgia tap tap on sheets of tin
so the rain's wrung clothes to rope on the line
I *day* this summer all defy
I kite song stutter dumb a cheap suitcase
a Hoyle deck tommy gun
the backyard siren is weirdly white Miss Anita O'Day
her pleasant rasp the scratch of a cracked glass lamp
a backhanded compliment courtesy kumquat and motor oil
and cedar shelf of jelly jars monstrous with moth and firefly
my zoo stirred to luminous
wind-whipped sheets snap from pins
garments ghost loose to the yard
I silk citrus sky I sublime ink in milk
tar pitch pouring now eliminates scent and cutie-cats from the scene
why I collect my cards
why I go inside
and Miss Anita O'Day doesn't lie (much)
mulch and mastication for jungle womb
the siren asks from the basin of her spun glass well
a well-spun glass she who asks sweeps acres silent
I commit rituals of colonization and play crazy eights
the cackle in these tatters
is that I knew them to be true

ONYX ARCADIA

If lucky — inversion — one wave back,
retracted, infinite claw set against tide.
This weave-water — lucent sheet over, under —
flat physic and cure.
The signal transmission of that planet
shouts down heaven and spectacle.
Slingshot sun and off — elsewhere —
code creased like tracery paper.
By the jetties' walk, whole oceans volute —
two worlds, this singular station —
elsewhere impossible, elsewhere war.

CONVENTION CENTERS OF THE NEW WORLD

They got too many hotels up on one end of Canal Street.
It don't make no sense.

Cause sooner or later that son-of-a-bitch is going to sink
in the Mississippi River because there are too many hotels!

Because they took all our dollar stores and ten cent stores
to build all those damn hotels. I don't know why.

They have property in New Orleans. Those people knew
something was wrong with their levee.

They're promising you things, but then when you get there,
it's gone, they ran out, or –

They sit on their hands and they didn't do nothing about it.
Nothing. They just sit and sit and sit.

It just made me feel like, you were waiting,
you were gonna let all those unfortunate people just die.

I don't know why.
The place was just expecting us to be wiped out.

IT'S THE BOLD NEW CITY OF THE SOUTH

c'mon now the bold new city of the south *loves* the black man

like weather-watchers love a storm

so replace **tornado** with **black man**

"when a black man strikes your home the results can be devastating"

"trailer parks are particularly vulnerable to a black man"

"unbelievably, that summer afternoon saw five separate black men
     touch down"

that is the bold new city of the south

even the nice whites of the bold new city of the south still wonder

what does the black man *want?*

has the black man lost his damn *mind?*

"this is perfect weather for a black man"

"despite advances in warning technology the black man will always
     be with us"

DRIFTGLASS

Vessels, missiles, her glass-cracking love letters.
That shade-hole up in the sky suggests the fate

of all the stones she's thrown, stuck in circles,
consigned to lesser lights, showboat satellite.

Her arm's script, sudden, Shakespearean.
Her shot makes sand and ordinary orchids new.

Her armament's igneous, erosion, or accident,
all fragments now, all secrets shed by the salt-lamp,

a trash of stones, that moon. Bright coat
finely-woven, now battered by shade.

A slow toe-trace of the island after winds
reveals a litter of milky stones, which returned

to water blue back to glass. *Brown bottle
for bark beer, green glass for well-water!*

Her day lengthens with broken windows and boy-oaths.
Her shards scratch, warp and wear, darken and double.

Her glass valentines smash the big dumb moon.
Some boys she stuns numb, lunar.

She hides in one word's flinty unfurling.
Per her letter expires, she wears its words thin.

Her satchel's full of nothing now but these broken bits.
She grasps glass dust, tucks her fist under her chin,

falls asleep curled in a skiff dragged half-ashore.
From its water rise islands, her shoulder and hip.

Drowned in the boat's womb, she may yet live,
if water will resolve, not solve, finish, not forgive.

knights of babylon and chaos and hermes.

*

The acid tangles into strychnine knots.

We hallucinate hotels undulate like flags.

Be mute else our spell is marred.

We massage the poor ease of our spine.

Some white lady asks to buy the hair right off your head.

Those sheaves' twenty years.

Raw knots, worshipful.

Not even for *Locks of Love?*

Blunt fall, we shave our necks for severance and excruciation.

Some of us present are worse than devils.

No matter, since we feel.

get cuttin', cracker, get goin'

DOWN SALUTE

Ownerless – without flag. We rest
pregnant, hold full of fish, their eyes
still focused. Mere fog – man in a cap,
man in fingerless gloves –
why do I accrete more than spice
as I sit, bundled in winter wool.
Mist and motion telegraph the scent –
why do I continue to shave in the convex
bowl of a copper pot or slip on a deck
slick with blood and scales – to write
"today he masters a pistol."

FIRST PERSON SHOOTERS

We run across the gates and down the fire escape.

We flutter under its iron eaves.

Summer's slowed our city, tarred down its gears.

Summer's overheated our city's machine.

We step from the ladder to the asphalt.

Guns distend our garments.

Sewn through pockets, lead shells rest next to the gun's bore.

We shoot at the city's sum, aim at everything.

We vault the sea wall, we strip.

Rust stains our discarded boots, sand collects in our shirts.

Warble at the waves that crack around our backs.

We carry subcutaneous radio under the trains and into the brine.

In our ears hum the tiniest glass receivers, opalescent silicate itch.

Ridiculous leisure, golden.

Ravenous, raucous, we turn our heads in time, we tune.

Solar shine, that, corona's tone a cure.

Each wave and ray, also parcel and particulate.

We are ravenous, we are raucous, we are sick.

We fall backwards into the blood-warm sea.

PACIFISM

took his jaw with chains

took his cheekbones with chains

his man-pretty, his *aw darlin:*

for stripper, for Shelly, for rigorous self-righteous

for I fucking *fucking* felt like it

posse, deputy, sad-ass superhero: my provisional micro-society

duly deputized by futureless and who was paying attention anyway

made you cry, cracker

honest officer I've never taken pleasure in the suffering of others

but god *bless* my icy delight at your shattering, charlatan

and god *bless* words

stupid fucking words, professor

who is full of talk

who has a head full of words

I slept via the agency of sweet soul music, of *revenger's chanteuse*

I slept via long hot shower, clean sheets, my bartender's discount

I slept with dowel and machete, no joke

I slept like a lolling baby, like the lullaby itself

that jackass not first or last

just the most *movie*, the most *glad theatrical*

Goddamn I'd go at any boy in any bar who used the c-word

who looked at me cross-eyed

I knew no *now* then

but I *broke* that boy – sent his sad ass back to Slidell –

yet here I am, here it is!

and you, fool, just sitting there, salacious –

even now I must remind myself not to kill you

SINGLE STATES

All darkened moon-glass —
black pebbles the channel of my errand.
Blood silt — rich through my teeth.
Waves hum down — sound indistinguishable
from stone — stones pulled through my hands.
Water — equally stone and glass —
infinite count of shot.
The rattle of waves drawn from rock —
cascade and stumble with weight.
Shore and wave the same substance —
fluid and solid, same.

SCIENCE-HORROR OF THE BLACK SEMINOLES

"Kill the brain, and you kill the ghoul."

Send in the broken, come on, boys —

Point at what's past and past animation and say nothing but *aw
he's dead he's all messed up.*

Go into grass, into marshlight matinee, go after that
and for what-all.

Are not our dead men meant to be unfeeling?

But when we regard our unassimilated armies
who's afraid of whom.

What unfeeling-ness equals *ah* annihilation.

To fear what? *Surely chill surely unreal.*
Some's come hanging and some's come horror.

Up the hill, dead men, strong as you are, shambles now.
What unfeeling-ness equals *ah wait*

ain't men are they even men anymore

Except for the truth of the thing, that they fought to a standstill
every manjack set against them.

Murderer's melody, who's for rooting for whom?

Must have caused a proper panic, that dead men prosper
while soldiers sink in canal, crevasse seeded with razorgrass –

oh damnation damnation.

Undead army from sea island breaker to gulf breaker,
clamdigger & cutlass –

Fought from no-place to no-place. Forgotten.

Pine cabin-in-the-woods and whitegirl.

I'll tell you they went in after them and never came out again –

Went down after and never came back –

CONVENTION CENTERS OF THE NEW WORLD

We had to sleep in the streets.
Not on the sidewalks, in the streets.

Cause the sidewalks was full of urine
and body waste, dead bodies.

And we had to sleep out there,
in the hell of waste and the dead bodies.

I walked from water up to my neck
to get to the Convention Center.

There was dead dogs, dead rodents,
you had to push all that kind of mess out of the way,

hoping that it didn't touch you.
I was pushing them out the way,

so many dead bodies coming from the Ninth Ward
up our way and they had people that was drowned up my way.

Now this Convention Center wasn't nothing nice,
I kid you not.

People still crying and begging to go home.
There's nothing there.

You have no running water. You have no lights.
The place stinks. It's contaminated.

I've been there twice.
I died there, I died.

Me, my ten-year-old daughter, my sister
and her thirty-two-year-old son,

we lived out there seven days.
Five days we had no food. No water.

Every night and every day the military people
was throwing down on us

like we was a bunch of wild animals.
They was on a hunt to kill.

They killed one guy right there in front of us,
run over him with a police car

and then they shot the man and left him there.
They didn't cover him up or nothing

and the next day,
it was so hot out there,

when they did come to pick him up,
his body was stuck to the ground.

So I can understand you want to keep control
of the people,

but why have those people draw guns on children?
Women with babies in their stomachs.

Every time you look around we breaking and running,
trying to get into the Convention Center

and they're drawing guns on people like that.
I mean, it don't make no kinda sense.

They wouldn't let you leave.
You had to stay there.

Cause we smelled like – I'm serious –
because everybody was smelling the same way –

smelling like sewer, like shit, piss.
That was the scariest time of my life.

And we had to have that on us
because we ain't had no water, we ain't had no sewer.

There wasn't no limit on it because you had to scrub yourself
just to get the scent out of your skin

Because, like I said, they knew they have a lot of poor people
like myself don't have no transportation,

don't have no money.
Well I have a car but it got under the water.

Me, my ten-year-old daughter, my sister
and her thirty-two year-old son, we lived out there seven days.

We looked for her for an hour and thirty minutes
in the Convention Center.

Five days we had no food. No water.
I seen children die, I seen old people die,

I seen murders, I seen rapes.
I seen people murder people then cut their heads off.

We already knew that the killer people
were putting them in the icebox,

killing little children and raping little children.
The men, the looters, the people that was staying in there.

I am telling you, that was the most horriblest experience
I have ever seen in my life.

I seen the troops shoot people. They ride around with guns
almost like we was in a prison camp.

No, the place wasn't on fire. It was some children upstairs
playing with the fire extinguisher.

Like hell. And like I said, I never in my life grew up in a house
with millions of people.

You know, I've always had my own room, my own,
you know, my own, I was always – just –

In the Convention Center, the buses came in.
Every night. Every day they was telling us

"The buses is coming, the buses is coming."
The buses passed right there in front of us and kept going!

The people was there to see the buses so everybody run,
rushing the buses to get on the damn buses and get out of there.

Every day they was moving us around, go here, go there,
the buses is gonna meet you here, meet you there.

They was lying. There was never no buses, they was lying.
They was just making us tired. The had us in there to kill us.

We used to look up at the bridge and see all the buses
going that way to the Superdome,

or to the hospital, or to the people in those condos,
getting them all out of there and going back.

Buses going back again, buses leaving out New Orleans again.
That's how it was.

It was NOPD police
but it wasn't our regular district police.

These were special NOPD policemen.
We was running from place to place telling them,

"Oh, this person dead, that person dead."
They said, "Well we can't do nothing about no dead bodies.

Y'all just don't worry.
Y'all just try to get the fuck out of here."

They say, "Y'all go to the bridge.
The bus's going to pick you up on the bridge."

I think it was they job to send the National Guards
and the armored people in there

to make sure everybody was evacuated.
They left us out there for five, six, seven days.

We stayed on the bridge nine hours.
They didn't care about us.

The first thing they dropped into us was boxes of cigarettes.
Not food. Not water. Boxes of cigarettes.

Two hours later they drop us water. And half of it burst open
cause they was so high up when they dropped it.

Two hours after that they drop us some army food in a box
we got to pour water in to heat up.

We was hungry,
we had no other choice.

The news got us out. Not the National Guard, not the Mayor, not Blanco,
the news people is the only ones who got us out.

Channel 26 got me out. Channel 26.
The rest of them was there to kill us.

I got tired of Convention Centers. I wanted
to come the hell up out of that damn Convention Center.

zulu social aid and pleasure club.

*

Deceiver we dwell in this bare island.

redeemer when it comes to work we are sturdy by nature

but we have toiled on the skin of your country and found no use

trod traces older than you and our hunger now a powerful thing

time for us to become your body we will lay it down lord

sense your grin and gullet devour until our spirits untie

redeemer think of us our marriage ink my sister my wife

the motes of cast gold inside of us

the excitement in our rivers when we are full enough to receive you again

UNDINE

Undine swims out after eating,
a slippery fish, a little sinner.

She trusts in spirits who are simply trouble,
who buoy her buoyant, float her like a bubble.

Her girl-gods mean fathoms and shapes
that know all about her wasted time.

Her girl-gods include the underwater man,
shatterer of ships, plague of fleets, resolute

foe of Francophones. The backswing
of the underwater man's ax blues copper,

splits sails, breaks boats back to timber.
The underwater man unchains spirits

to have them befuddle sailors, blacken masts
with lightning, woo mosquitoes malarial.

Little undine swims out in his liquid lavage,
and she knows there are dead men down there,

armymen, sailormen, marines and legionnaires.
She writhes through seaweed, she speeds.

The admiral's leather-bound books sank
long ago, moldered now, those records and rules.

She's schooled, as her uncles say, but prefers
divination. Underwater man's daughter.

She don't heed lessons, she don't take care.
Her uncles whistle her back to shore

but she pretends to grow fins and gills.
If she can swim, she will. If she wills, she will.

stop the floating piano
so we can see its insides
& who could be playing it
stop the supernature
godawful its ragtime tide its
me with nothing
spoon ring or twine
lessen a pigeon head
let's credit a good arm
rest on that headstone
we could flag it down
that piano devil man
all the girls sing
are you-all shitting me
with the ring and the string
that girl requested
set your hammers aside
tell me what I've done
quickly now behold
the whole world

she wants in it
its bullfrog balloonery
likely a mister devil man
or the ass-backwards river
dumb-hearted dirty
but pockets
no cheap glass heart
trapped in tinfoil still
a hardworking skeleton
lady
with palm fronds instead
in spats and pegged trousers
who? then *ah!*
I describe circles
I make altar of the empty-headed
attendez-moi, miniature devils
devils whistle and witness
how the scrap strikes you
before the piano eddies away
thus far

YOU'RE IT

Hello my name is Mississippi   my name is Slim   Blind

                    Uncle   I'm Junior   Red

Ivory   T-Bone my name is Fiddling   Sonny Boy

          Joe   I know two thousand tunes

EIGHT PIECE

Slipped notes. Once our brass sang —
where the dock spilled — now I
waste hours on a string — piano gestures
smaller than a hand count. Each port —
a chorus. Each quay a caesura.
Something about drunkenness on flat land —
only some fools call it grace —
once I read you cannot fold a flood.
Nights all I hear is scrap and slice —
and whistle welcomes. Good of us —
to recollect a wind instrument.

X   Y   Z

Did you say your mother fled from wild pigs
My mother fled from wild pigs too.

Did you say your mother set her schoolhouse on fire
My mother set hers on fire too.

When Jack-a-long and Jil-a-croix go down the hill
to fetch a pail of water, the hill is water and the well is water

and so's the pail. Water's the battery, the best.
Boy-jack's hot copper and sister-Jill, a transistor.

And besides they went for licorice & vacuum tubes & pipettes,
capillary action to suck the scarlet right from their fingertips.

Will you be my blood brother   What if you have diseases.
Please, pirouettes, for she's a pirate. And planks for you-know-what.

Pirogue, & Pontius Pilate, & wash your hands if you touch that.
What kind of pigs   Peccary pigs why do you ask.

You heifer. You manatee. You cow of the land. You cow of the sea.
Aquacow. Terracow. You dumb thing, poorer than pork.

When they go down the hill the hill's a wave
and the boy and girl are pail, bucket, port, and bay.

Princelings for prizefights. Pliers & piers & piercings & puncture.
Philistines, & phosphorous, & phlebotomy,

which it says here is also known as venesection, pretty name,
the act and practice of opening a vein.

And pigments; her mudcake and his mudcake, their bakery.
I'll teach you your alphabet backwards so repeat after me.

My tongue's all funny but I want to say those words you said.
ooo   vay   dublavay   eeks   egreeks   zed

BARON SAMEDI'S ADDRESS TO MODERN LOVERS

Delight-bearing in all your media.
Belt up for neither hope nor hysteria.

But if heck-bent, take meridian magnolias
and make discipline from syllables,

strange as street names and as mutable.
Master both pleasant and ghastly,

gauge leisure by what it affords or affronts.
Delight: a fistfight between midwives,

to drag such a thing into the world. What if
upon asking me what might make delight,

the answers allow a revolver emptied
into a Christmas crowd, or to pierce a saint,

burn Ursulines and her sisters to the ground?
Simple abuse and simple delight.

Form elemental finery from feather and fin
and what gown have you dumbly undone?

Have none of it, temptation tethered
to carriages where horses abound.

Bless every castle and shack. The least phial's
a fire, is it not? Every opera reckons a fen.

Inhale and expire. Handle and dismantle.
What furious luck beckons each bounty!

They create new ambiguities and mutual guilt
but of specters there are none. Delight.

A graveyard, a monocle, an orchestra,
a top hat, a doctor, and love in Christ.

SPENT LETTER

Who said "mawkish gods" – oh
that is true and still comic –
all done now or close to it. Done with color
and doubly done with sound –
whispers – to start with.
Coming up on fraction, tip of ice
or bit of tropic – whispers, then moans.
Next narrow exit: rivers. And indigo
again. It's a pity we don't have hold
for history books – it's a tune –
this is why no darling, no diary.

rex.

*

Eenie meenie minie moe

catch the nigger by her toe

if she holler let her go

If you now beheld us your affections would become tender.

Our riddle-doze, handle our riddle, unfinished.

A thin mist falls on us, yet our shape, invisible, we retain.

Finally starts to rain and now everything takes molasses.

Our fingers, spread to nets, catch rain –

we anoint our foreheads with droplets.

Feast before renunciation.

We draw our hands across our cheeks and laugh.

Riches fall on us, violet and green.

Parades, those tired monsters crawl along.

Torches set to brass and drum.

Illuminate a heaven laced with dimes and crickets.

Beauty, a shawl flung over us, the riot.

Of two most rare affections heavens rain grace

LANDSCAPE WITH CITRUS

Lovely smoke and orange oil
scratched into their skin.

FM hiss in her teeth as the ladybug steps
from his nipple to her fingertip,

dumb delay that defines the mysteries.
Answer to the question *what were you doing* –

moving mirrors through the grove.
Moon tilts in the flat sea between them

as they climb to the city of spiders.
What happens to her? But he –

this is much more than bad luck –
descends through the branches

to the tart static of radio sparking
from her teeth and fingernails.

Like the mirror, she follows.
Silver-backed glass fractures and falls

down past tiers of reflected fruit.
The duplicate trace delayed, somehow base.

The tableau elicits fiction, false reports
of all their turbulence, its plumage.

But the bower's aperture *does* open.
They *do* collapse to radio notes.

No shield from the science, so see it —
they scroll down, they split moon —

they kiss then shatter. Motion's norm,
peculiar to their living and falling form.

thoth.

*

Hither for stale to catch these thieves!

No few psychomagicians, these.

As a sailor knows her craft so the fletcher bends taut to a half-moon
and kisses the feather.

Shirtlessness our specialty, we sit prim at the stern.

You are supposed to compliment me on my outfit

We pull pins of bent steel from our hair, lockpickers and lords.

Come, hang us.

Canvas shuffles the falling sail.

Peeled free of it we curl lissome and arch, stand nutmeg
in the equatorial sun, we turn.

This is my starboard and this is my port

Around the world let's go around the world.

Directions spoken here and here clear, as stars and cards.

Sea pulled out, spooling loose, unreeling weight of the sea.

Let's dress in black flags, play the game of daggers
the game of hearts.

To marry you, that would be like protecting yourself from the cold
by setting yourself on fire —

A sulfur barometer.

That could control the moon, make flows and ebbs.

That could perpetuate, not harbor, not bay.

What is it with you and these moons?   *These vapid moons?*

SHOOT THE MOON

We murmur through the slough.

Defectors, we wash in salt, the Atlantic bisects us.

Our hair burnishes to rust, to russet.

Near drunken, boiled in our beds, poisoned with sun.

Numbed by the broad-watered god who handled our bones,

who burned our wax to its wick.

For days, we shave shards of ice from squares of ice, eat ice alone.

We play hearts, the cards' colors faded to bluish tattoos.

Their edges fray to open pages.

Else we lust for the icon and the ink of the sacred heart.

Our hearts marked, stung red, stung russet.

Blinds billow, embellish the jalousie.

White waves adorn and destroy the shore.

proteus.

*

Make us strange stuff.

We narrate.

We romance but you romaticize. We err but you eroticize.

We spit and say sorry.

Even within tropics' fog, we see our own breath.

We walk on the moon.

South, southern.

All those strangers' evil apples and hats made out of hay.

Drugged, our kiss becomes acidic and then we say something.

I just don't rightly recollect

It tastes like honey, words stuck like mud in our sibling-head.

Jade, now the color of dinosaurs sucked heavy into the bog.

That deep and dreadful organ-pipe pronounced:

Time to be home soon. Time for moon.

Almighty God, I declare.

Make us strange stuff.

Almighty God I tell you what.

DARE YOU

Here's a blown bouquet, lady: bad chance, my inheritance.
Whistle out if my colloquial don't make no sense.

Athleta christi all around the yard, race you from bulkhead
to bamboo stand. *You're* a bulkhead, bamboo boy:

sticks and twigs all knit up with tendon. I'll wrestle you for it,
I'll haggle you down, name-brand. I'll bargain-basement you.

Ah, y'all! Shirt-shirking, short-shucking skinny-dippers!
And the dreamy chlorine and the stray rain and the very air:

all media equal in heat, distinct only by weight, womb-warm.
Our obstacl'd course hazards mudpits and sinkholes,

tire swings and actual alligators and trees seething with fire ants.
I can make it   Chicken fighter you know you can't   Yes I can

And well late-on midnight moony Jack Naught jumps
off the St. Mark's bridge, his spindly limbs dis-splayed.

Splasher and paddler and I can see you but you can't see me,
the pasty-pale scarecrow crows – oh ho ho ho, ah hee hee hee.

If your best friend jumped off the St. Mark's bridge, would you?
It'll go where it go, yo. She wouldn't skunk me if she could.

She stands the scarecrow and mounts the mister locks her head
to his wet neck and jerks herself to giggles against his skinny hips.

Now this shit is the weirdest shit there is, warrior & practical joker.
The floor is water it's okay we are failing the claim (truly)

we don't know what it is but superimpose me on your stride (again)
where we've never been, hien? What were y'all thinking, times ten.

In wickedness the twins catch hard the big stick of do-hell.
Might as well   I will if you will   but I'll never tell.

WARP WATER

Port home squats parallel —
its rust irons stretch to the horizon's lid —
along its walls children chase and tease.
Sea sluiced through fortification gates —
metal yards wedged into walls and barnacles.
The market — nets of onions —
tomatoes in bins. All my brothers wait
for the wave — sunlights shine
on the pearl's crest — my mates
look up from their cinnamon coffee — shake
stings from their hands — drown.

CONVENTION CENTERS OF THE NEW WORLD

A lot of people know that I'm emotionally disturbed,
and they know it don't take much to upset me.

This old lady that was my neighbor for like fourteen years,
every time I used to get upset, she used to come and see about me.

She used to always tell me, "Pray." Which I always do.
That's pretty much that's how it is.

My sister live, I'd say, eight, ten blocks from where I was living.
So by the time I decided to put something in a bag go by her

and cook, I go downstairs to get something out my deep freezer,
and it was floating. Say, Lord, have mercy!

Still I'm not paying no attention. I'm thinking "The storm passed!"
Cause this is the day after the storm.

Right before all of this happened, I'd been studying the Bible,
reading it.

In a sense it kind of makes you waive your faith, you know,
is this really real, or, you know sometimes, you wish that –

I would've been better off if I would've drowned, or?
This is – we're living in hell, pure hell, and it's just unfair.

It's just unfair to me. I mean, I have so much unfinished business
in New Orleans, that – will it ever get taken care of?

Will the pieces ever get put together?
Will I be spending the rest of my life living in the past?

You know, what? Where do I go from here?
Where do my children go from here?

And as you see, my kids are very intelligent kids.
Where do we go from here?

You know, now, you know, do I have to raise my kids
sleeping on a bench or living in our car

hoping that somebody assists me, gives me some kinda help?
I mean, where do we go from here?

I just feel like, the government has really, really failed us.
It's just unreal.

I think it go all the way back.
But it's like the evilness in New Orleans, it go all the way back.

You know the first thing they say, if something happen,
if they got a crime, you don't run.

You just lay down wherever you at,
or you stay wherever you at.

I didn't pay it no mind.
I look and I see.

I think the government failed us. I think the mayor failed us,
I think the government failed us. I think our president failed us.

Like I say, you just don't know because you wasn't there.
Nobody knows what we went through but God himself and us.

I just had to show them that they could not move me.
I had to fight. I fought. I fought. I fought.

That's pretty much that's how it is. Every person
from New Orleans, their family has been there.

I could pray but whatever God want to hand me,
He gonna want to hand me.

Some good people come from New Orleans, but it's just the way
they train people in New Orleans, I guess.

They can't give us enough money to replace what they took.
They can't. They can't do nothing to replace what was took.

They can't do nothing to compensate us.
I guess that's all I got to say. That's it.

That really hurt me. I've been arrested a lot of times for fighting
which you knew I was guilty.

But this time I was really innocent,
and that hurt my heart.

This was a foster lady I was staying with,
she never did feed me.

I remember when I first got there,
the social worker introduced me to her,

and I'm like, Wow, I got a family. As soon as the social worker left,
I told the lady, I said, "I'm hungry."

And the lady just fixed me a bowl of white rice, with nothing else.
I asked, "Where's the chicken?"

It was the kind of stuff that goes on in New Orleans.
Alright. I paid out for everything I got. I'm done.

YOU EATEN YET?

outside, the cloud kings, the faces found in palm-fruit

pinched face shocked face

inside, granddad's hole in the wall serves ground pork

and ground beef

special meals for special friends

but in *my* kitchen

corn kernels corn meal cast iron silvered for grinding

I cannot get it fine enough is this fine enough

we can't live here we can't live here anymore

UNDINE, DETAIL

My suitor's the sea but I'll only be
the bride of a sailorman.

Isn't this analog world good enough
for Agwe, who dresses like Aquaman?
Doesn't Agwe ride on a great purple seahorse?

No, he drives an atom-powered submarine
that bristles with laser guns.

Angry Agwe will boil the sea to coral.
Angry as a pufferfish stiff with quarrel.
Then the sunken spires will be sharp as spines,
a sound city for a girl made of brine.

MATRIMONY

Newly anointed, dried with salt.
He will tug into this shirt, his counter-man,

his evident armor, while she claims
one day we are going to put this all away.

She caresses this crease, the perfect cross,
right where his sternum sits.

Only the mister's muscle pulls
his shirt to approximate skin.

A spent spirit abides here, flush
with his shoulder's square, his flesh.

Numb now, but once a whole man,
gaunt but still somehow glad.

A chambered man, tender innards
compressed by welts and worn.

His anatomy no accident, though marred
thereby: thorn and thistle in his fingerprints.

The texture by which she knows his hand
now carnage, for all it's cast prettily.

His mass wearies her, a welding
more than a wedding, bound not bonded.

No cold to quell the man, no work.
Nor gorge or gulley to swallow his mass.

The washing's done, the drying begun,
threadbarren hung from wire to wire.

The phone line will fray and unspool.
The island will fall beneath the sea.

CODE NOIR

Slept for thirty years to remember him.
Her words, swollen to seed pearls.

Slept to rest her head in this man's lap,
to trust his trust, his exhausted trance,

to loose her hair's black sash
without consequence. The backstage hush

of *The Tempest* ("their theatre
is quite savage"), its sets of jetsam.

Slept thirty years to dismiss
this audience, this black book,

all that is not their speech,
oxygen bought with hurricanes.

The hours before their child awakes.
That boy will fancy illusions and lies,

tricks driven by what cannot be known,
their prior bodies, her collarbone, his hip,

limited hinge, joint by which fixed,
the elastic ache of their sex

as they think of her son asleep.
Are enclosures all that are clear?

Years become the length of years.
She walked to the remains of Paris

on the wreck of fourteen thousand ships
just to return to this patchwork:

the mercy of their revenge,
the nothing their privacy takes.

EVERYONE COME

Lace and crash notwithstanding.
Spurs corrupt steps —
for dancers' deck.
Some steel — just air and iron —
seals the rent flesh shut.
We celebrate ourselves insensate.
Crucible steel, rings and nods —
silence good as I do.
Artless parlance, still —
occupying the same, displaced,
in your floating iron, I do.

TERRARIA

rocks and weeds and
birds and bugs
both the creeping and the graven
cataract and rat and
man o' war and banana
shadepole! salamander! skink!
come preserve us in your haven

GENEALOGY OF JADES

To make a garden the colors all called jade.

And jade itself calls from the greenhouse.

darling

By jade the artisan's marble, broken.

By jade the colonial tile reduced to dust.

Verb tropic, to move in martial coordination.

In jade the allowance of avian echo, one hundred open throats.

Aperture and carving stick, jade bled to the haze.

Jade an occupation, a folded letter, *here take this*

Jade exposes a room to southern sunlights.

We sleep on grass floors we sleep on our back

Jade tints the jagged half-coin, the sun-hot profit.

Make a welcome, jade, of ruiner to ruin.

Jade tastes the question *are you in?*

And the answer: inside as out, outside as in.

A fingertip rounds the glass to make the shape sing.

Mouth ringed with lime. Vice as the origin of vice.

Wicked, deliberate jade, arsenic and bonbon.

Jade, poison's blush and origin.

A jade cell's ambition both stiff and supple.

Jade, the telling of which is betrayal.

Garden glass cracked now, a flock of hammers there –

Each flower's finger folds into the palm, nightshade turns in.

Each finger wets the petal over the jade bulb.

Jade the mouth ringed with lime sweet the word tasting sweet.

Jade seed, a second.

Jade pearl unfurls the garden, by which we recognize texture.

We obtain in the satin of your mouth.

HAULING OUT

Gone from this for months – once
I called it vintage, the attic evident
riches because we had no basement –
nor could – you wore the lilac of it
as well as some corset – some
would say tragic mulatta, split-stayed
by daylight time, water time – forgetting
all the grotesque wealth of life, even
in attics and windows – and tragediennes,
petulant. No: the liquid stays
indolent. A lizard, evolved from emeralds.

FEVER OF THE DIVINE

oh aye you slung me in sails you carried me

the heat's sheen dissolved distance

that heat approached all my oddments and ends

all my surface left to sun

solar shine, that, corona's tone a cure

perimeter shine, my ensoulment, my emulsion

from that sailor's sheet: oh blue-black of sky evacuated

you carried me

white of the sheet's weave as well

I asked of fevers out of fevers:

relieve or release

and undiseased, unlapsed, you laughed, you gasped:

gods

there is but one heaven, lover, no other need

the host that is sunken, and its colors, these

TRANSFIX INGREDIENT

this little jade claw undoes all

the flanks of the lizard flare

palette and shade, its wizardry

curl of chameleon claw green in a screen door's solder fix

ozone scent sunk to wire tines

signature animal, its cold blood done folding now

thunder trills the reptile, those airs shared chameleon

green-god, green teeming, leaves also sheath

throat swollen scarlet

white paint open the door, cut a way through this stray rain

sprung open, each spring-cut sound

liar's library & boning knife, color & kin

persistent, the world of grasses, of drown

our plundered underworld

saltwater, our skin

NOTES AND ACKNOWLEDGMENTS

Thanks to my parents, brother, sisters, aunts, uncles, cousins, neighbors, co-religionists, arch-foes, victims, allies, and members of the Justice League, Panhandle franchise, and/or the Legion of Doom: from Jeremie to Little Haiti, from Jupiter to Neptune Beach, from Tallahassee to Wakulla, from Tuscaloosa to Houma, from New Orleans to Gulfport.

My thanks to Charlotte Boulay, Jesmyn Ward, Karyna McGlynn, and Nickole Brown for aid and inspiration.

Thanks to Allan, Chris, Linda, Molly, Esther and the friends of Coffee House Press.

Thanks to Rae Armantrout and Lorna Goodison.

The last line of "Down Salute" is taken from a poem by Medbh McGuckian.

The first line of "Science-Horror of the Black Seminoles" is from George Romero's *Night of the Living Dead*, as is the line about being dead, being all messed up.

Many thanks to Amanda Reichert for the details of "X Y   Z" and for much else besides.

The nursery rhyme reference in the poem "rex." is now usually heard as "catch a tiger by his toe." However, this is not its exclusive version; here, I've simply restored the rhyme to its awful origins.

In "Dare You" the term *athleta christi* refers to a class of early Christian martyrs, the most popular of whom is St. Sebastian, who I mention elsewhere.

The Code Noir, decreed by Louis XIV in 1685, defined the terms of slavery in the French colonies, and also prohibited the practice of any religion other than Roman Catholicism.

Several lines of the book are taken from Shakespeare's *The Tempest*.

COLOPHON

Saltwater Empire was designed at Coffee House Press,
in the historic warehouse district of downtown Minneapolis.
The text is set in Garamond.

FUNDER ACKNOWLEDGMENTS

Coffee House Press is an independent nonprofit literary publisher.
Our books are made possible through the generous support of grants
and gifts from many foundations, corporate giving programs, state and
federal support, and through donations from individuals who believe
in the transformational power of literature. Coffee House Press
receives general operating support from the Minnesota State Arts
Board, through an appropriation by the Minnesota State Legislature
and from the National Endowment for the Arts, and major general
operating support from the McKnight Foundation, and from Target.
Coffee House also receives support from: an anonymous donor; the
Elmer and Eleanor Andersen Foundation; the Buuck Family
Foundation; the Patrick and Aimee Butler Family Foundation;
Jennifer Haugh; Stephen and Isabel Keating; Allan and Cinda
Kornblum; Mary McDermid; Stu Wilson and Melissa Barker; the
Lenfestey Family Foundation; Rebecca Rand; the law firm of
Schwegman, Lundberg, Woessner, P.A.; the James R. Thorpe
Foundation; the Woessner Freeman Family Foundation; the Wood-
Rill Foundation; and many other generous individual donors.

This activity is made possible
in part by a grant from the
Minnesota State Arts Board,
through an appropriation by the
Minnesota State Legislature
and a grant from the National
Endowment for the Arts. MINNESOTA
STATE ARTS BOARD

TARGET.

To you and our many readers across the country,
we send our thanks for your continuing support.

Good books are brewing at coffeehousepress.org